THE *Little Book* OF

~

MONET

~

A REFRESHING LOOK
AT THE BEST OF
MONET'S PAINTINGS

DEDICATION
For Bunchie

Editor: Fleur Robertson
Editorial Assistance: Nicola Dent, Laura Potts, Jillian Stewart
Original Design Concept: Peter Bridgewater, Nigel Duffield
Design: Jill Coote
Picture Research: Leora Kahn
Director of Production: Gerald Hughes
Typesetting: Julie Smith

MALLARD PRESS
An imprint of BDD Promotional Book Company, Inc.,
666 Fifth Avenue, New York, NY 10103.
Mallard Press and its accompanying duck logo
are trademarks of the BDD Promotional Book Company, Inc.,
registered in the U.S. Patent and Trademark Office, Copyright © 1992

CLB 3141
© 1992 Colour Library Books Ltd, Godalming, Surrey, England.
First published in the United States of America in 1992 by The Mallard Press.
Printed and bound in Singapore.

ISBN 0-7924-5815-X

THE *Little Book* OF
MONET

RICHARD DAWES

MALLARD
PRESS

Introduction

Monet did not invent Impressionism single-handedly, but it is his pictures that most readily spring to mind when we think of this movement: works like *Wild Poppies*, *Impression: Sunrise* and *Blue Waterlilies*. In a career spanning some seventy years he painted genteel portraits, busy street scenes, sunlit landscapes, cathedrals, rivers and the sea and, finally, waterlilies that bordered on the abstract. He moved between town and country, from abject poverty to comparative ease, from obscurity to international fame, but throughout his long life his sole and constant aim was to capture on canvas a single moment in the unending play of light.

Claude Monet was born in Paris on 14 November, 1840. When he was five the family moved to Le Havre, where his father went into the wholesale grocery business with his brother-in-law. The boy drew from an early age and by the time he was fifteen he was known locally for his caricatures, which he was quick to sell – a pastime from which Monet made a considerable sum of money during his adolescence. At eighteen he was introduced to outdoor painting by the Le Havre artist Eugène Boudin, and before long the latter's revolutionary ideas and the beauty of the Normandy countryside had inspired him to devote his life to landscape painting.

In 1859 Monet went to study in Paris, where he met Pissarro. Then, after returning from a brief period of military service in Algeria, the young artist found that the ideas of the painter Jongkind had a great influence on his early development. Working in Gleyre's studio in Paris for two years from 1862, Monet mixed in a milieu that led to his meeting the greatest painters of the time: Sisley, Renoir, Courbet, Cézanne, Whistler and Manet.

At the start of his career, in 1865 and 1866, Monet had his paintings accepted by the Salon and began to sell some of his work. The sort of work liked by the critics, though, was not really the kind that Monet wanted to paint. Persisting with his reviled "Independent" style instead, Monet remained desperately poor for years, particularly after the birth of his son Jean in 1867 and his marriage to Camille Doncieux in 1870, events which alienated his family.

Impression: Sunrise, painted at Le Havre, was the now famous picture that gave its name to Impressionism when it was shown in 1874, at the first exhibition by a group of radical young painters who saw Monet as their leader. The term "Impressionism" was coined by a critic to deride Monet, and the group in general, but they came to see its appropriateness and the name stuck.

Monet's reputation continued to grow throughout the 1870s, for most of which time he lived at Argenteuil, on the Seine, where he painted hundreds of river scenes. In 1883 he settled at Giverny, where, having lost his wife in 1879, he set up home with Alice Hoschedé. Together they brought up his two sons and her six children by her late husband, the art collector Ernest Hoschedé. At Giverny Monet was later to create a magnificent flower garden and a water garden that was to provide inspiration throughout the last thirty years of his life.

From the 1890s Monet adopted a new approach to his subjects, producing the *Grain Stacks, Poplars, Rouen Cathedral, London* and *Venice* series, before devoting himself almost exclusively to the monumental *Waterlilies* series, The latter occupied him, despite the handicap of his failing eyesight, until his death at the age of eighty-six on 5 December, 1926.

Although he had no formal art training, no encouragement from most of his family and received little but ridicule from the critics for much of his early career, throughout his life Monet persevered with an almost superhuman determination and belief in his work. As a result, he gave the world some of the most successful attempts made by any painter to transform the fleeting aspects of nature into art.

Le Déjeuner sur l'herbe

Manet's painting with the same title had caused a scandal in 1863 by showing a naked woman sitting relaxed on the grass beside a fully clothed man. At the same time as paying Manet a compliment, Monet wanted to make his own impact – not by shock tactics but by painting a dozen life-sized figures, with great attention to detail, in *natural* light. No one had tackled such an ambitious subject before.

Both encouraged and disheartened by Courbet, who had some experience of large-scale canvases, Monet made sketches in the spring of 1865, one of which is seen here. He never finished the huge painting itself, but gave it to his landlord in 1877 as a security against rent he owed. When he got it back seven years later it had been ruined by damp, and only two fragments have survived.

1865 (dated 1866)
51" x 73"
Oil on canvas
Pushkin Museum, Moscow

Lady in the Garden

This beautiful painting is of the garden of Monet's aunt and the lady in the title is Jeanne-Marguerite Lecadre, his cousin. Monet's mother died in 1857, followed soon after by Jacques Lecadre, the brother-in-law and partner of Monet's father, Alphonse. The Monet family moved into the Lecadre home in Le Havre and Alphonse asked the widowed Marie-Jeanne Lecadre to take the teenage Monet in hand, as he had become difficult since losing his mother. Recognizing his talent at drawing, Marie-Jeanne encouraged Monet to be an artist. It was to be a hard road for all concerned. Ten years later, at the time of this work, Monet's common-law wife, Camille, was pregnant and living in Paris, denounced by Monet's family and temporarily abandoned by Monet, who had been forced to return home due to lack of money.

1867
32" x 39"
Oil on canvas
Hermitage, St. Petersburg

*C*amille

Having had two pictures accepted by the Salon in 1865 – the first time he had tried – Monet submitted two more the following year. Again the jury accepted both. One was a landscape, *The Road to Chailly*; the other was to have been the ground-breaking *Le Déjeuner sur l'herbe*. Realizing that he could not finish that in time, Monet abruptly changed tack, completing this life-sized study of Camille Doncieux in only four days. Probably the first picture for which Monet's nineteen-year-old mistress and future wife modeled (there were to be many more), the coquettish portrait was reviewed rapturously by the French novelist Emile Zola and later bought for a generous 800 francs by Arsène Houssaye, the discerning editor of the magazine *L'Artiste*.

1866
91" x 60"
Oil on canvas
Kunsthalle, Bremen

Women in the Garden

Determined to work entirely in the open air on this eight-and-a-half-foot-tall canvas, Monet lowered it on pulleys into a trench he had dug in the garden in order to reach the upper part. Other Impressionists dismissed this approach as gimmickry, but Monet remained true to his ideal. Camille, his young mistress, posed for the three grouped figures and possibly the fourth, in hired gowns – the same dresses, in fact, that are to be seen in the painting *Le Déjeuner sur l'herbe*.

Monet finished the canvas in Honfleur – only for the 1867 Salon to reject it. Luckily, Monet's friend, the painter Bazille, later bought it for 2,500 francs, paying Monet in monthly amounts of fifty francs. At the time, these instalments were often the only income Monet could hope for – critically damned, he rarely sold his work.

1866-7
104" x 82"
Oil on canvas
Musée d'Orsay, Paris

Claude Monet

The Magpie

After a spring in which his financial troubles led him to try to drown himself, Monet spent the autumn and winter of 1868 at Etretat, on the Normandy coast, with his mistress Camille and his son Jean, who had been born the previous summer. That winter Monet returned to a subject he held dear, and one in which he would find inspiration again and again over the years: the snowscape. True to his belief that landscape should be painted from life, Monet would work in all weathers, regardless of their severity – later in his career, while painting in Norway, he regularly endured temperatures of -25°F!

Despite its fresh, captivating beauty, it is thought that *The Magpie* was one of two paintings by Monet rejected by the Salon in 1869.

1868-9
31" x 51"
Oil on canvas
Musée d'Orsay, Paris

The Basin at Argenteuil

In 1872, on Manet's recommendation, Monet settled in the riverside village of Argenteuil. The older painter, who lived across the Seine at Gennevilliers, also picked out the house for Monet, not far from the water. Argenteuil was fast losing its rural character, but what Monet liked about it was the boats – the lifeblood of the place seemed to be the river.

Monet and Manet met almost daily, and together developed a new style of painting. Unmixed colors, boldly applied, captured the sun's effect on sky and water in an entirely new way. This picture is one of the many studies Monet made of the Seine, particularly in the first half of the 1870s. Clouds, boats and people alike seem to drift by on this peaceful Sunday afternoon.

1872
24" x 32"
Oil on canvas
Musée d'Orsay, Paris

Regatta at Argenteuil

Impressionism was born at Argenteuil, where Monet, Manet, and Renoir often met to paint and discuss painting. The Seine here was dead straight – an ideal stretch for racing sailing boats, and for watching them. This subject suited Monet perfectly too: again and again he strove to capture the excitement of slender boats with tall sails cutting through sparkling water.

This picture was among works bequeathed to the State in 1894 by Monet's wealthy friend and patron Gustave Caillebotte, who himself painted and had exhibited with the Impressionists for the first time in 1876. It probably appealed to Caillebotte because his house is the left of the two, and one of the figures is thought to be him.

1872
24" x 40"
Oil on canvas
Musée d'Orsay, Paris

The Luncheon

The meal over, Camille walks in the dappled sunlight with an unidentified guest, while Jean plays in the shade of the table. Of the garden pictures that Monet painted during his seven years at Argenteuil, this is the largest and the most impressive. It was bought by Gustave Caillebotte, the wealthy painter and collector, who, in 1894, bequeathed sixteen of Monet's canvases to the State, which accepted eight.

This is a scene of domestic tranquillity of the kind that Monet often took as his subject in the early years. It is interesting to note that, from their position as the focal point of the painting, the glass, the silver coffee pot, the fruit and the bread seem at least as important to Monet as his loved ones – in fact, throughout his life the artist was renowned for his delight in the pleasures of the table.

1873
63" x 79"
Oil on canvas
Musée d'Orsay, Paris

Impression: Sunrise

In the winter of 1873-4 Monet's constant money worries led him to propose a group exhibition of the "Independent" painters, of which he was one. This took place in the photographer Nadar's studio in April and May 1874, and drew scorn from the critics and public alike. One reviewer leapt on the title *Impression: Sunrise* – which Monet had chosen in haste – dubbing Monet an "Impressionist" and claiming that wallpaper was better finished than this painting. The name stuck and was soon seen by the artists to be an fitting way to describe the new movement.

A fine example of a painting of a single moment, Monet probably completed this study of Le Havre harbor in one morning. The work was stolen from the Musée Marmottan in 1985 and, despite police efforts, it remained missing for five years.

1873 (dated 1872)
20" x 25"
Oil on canvas
Musée Marmottan, Paris

Wild Poppies

Famous the world over and perhaps the best loved of all Impressionist paintings, this was among the 240 or so canvases Monet produced during his seven years at Argenteuil. The river, the village and the countryside surrounding this idyllic spot near Paris were all a rich source of inspiration and pleasure for Monet. With a good wife and a young son, and money suddenly flowing in from the sale of his paintings, the first two years at Argenteuil were a particularly happy time for Monet. Abundance and delight pour from this canvas, and Monet clearly felt it was a success since he included it in the first Impressionist exhibition, held in 1874. There it was sold to Jean-Baptiste Faure, a farsighted and enthusiastic collector of the artist's work.

1873
20" x 26"
Oil on canvas
Musée d'Orsay, Paris

The Boulevard des Capucines

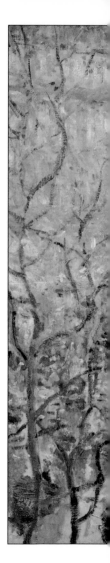

By painting people as crude blurs and splashes of color rather than as individuals, Monet split the critics with this picture. Louis Leroy, who poked fun at Monet's *Impression: Sunrise*, shown, like this work, at the first Impressionist exhibition in 1874, asked if someone could tell him just what the "innumerable black tongue-lickings" were in the bottom half of the picture. Others hailed the very vagueness of the figures as a clever way of suggesting the restless movement of swarming crowds. Monet certainly picked the right location: this view from the photographer Nadar's studio captures perfectly the rhythm of the busy heart of nineteenth-century Paris.

1873
24" x 32"
Oil on canvas
Pushkin Museum, Moscow

The Pond at Montgeron

Monet spent the second half of 1876 as the guest of Ernest Hoschedé at the Château de Rottenbourg at Montgeron, southeast of Paris. During this time the Belgian businessman, one of the earliest collectors of Impressionist paintings, commissioned a set of four decorative panels for his luxurious country house. In contrast to Monet's many pictures intended to capture the essence of contemporary life, there was nothing modern in subject matter about these. The fourth, undoubtedly the strongest, is this introspective study of the secluded pond in the grounds of the house. Only after looking twice do most people notice the figures Monet painted by the pondside.

1876-7
68" x 76"
Oil on canvas
Hermitage, St. Petersburg

La Gare Saint-Lazare

Renoir told the story that Monet, stung by the criticism that fog was an unsuitable subject for a picture, decided to give his critics something even murkier: a train belching out smoke and steam. Thinking that Monet was an artist of stature, the director of the railway company ordered the platforms to be cleared and the trains to be halted and stoked up to give off as much smoke as the artist wanted.

Between January and March 1877 Monet worked flat out, producing twelve canvases. Some he was forced to complete in his nearby studio, but this one he finished on the spot. Working at platform level, he caught the play of steam and smoke in the sunlight that filtered through the glass roof of this "cathedral of the machine age."

1877
30" x 41"
Oil on canvas
Musée d'Orsay, Paris

Rue Saint-Denis, 30 June 1878

Early in 1878, Monet and his family took a large apartment in a respectable part of Paris near the Parc de Monceau. From here he made trips to paint landscapes just outside the city, but his earlier fascination with street scenes was also rekindled.

The climax of the World's Fair, held in Paris in 1878, coincided with the public holiday on 30 June, and the city's streets were awash with bunting and flag-waving crowds. As he had done for *The Boulevard des Capucines* five years earlier, Monet painted the festivities in the Rue Saint-Denis from a balcony, only this time he draws the viewer right into the sea of color, as if with a zoom lens. So energetically did he work that he completed two pictures of the scene that day.

1878
30" x 20"
Oil on canvas
Musée des Beaux-Arts, Rouen

$\mathcal{H}$aystack near $\mathcal{G}$iverny

By April 1883, when he began to rent a house in Giverny, on the Seine northwest of Paris, Monet had a greatly extended family. Camille had died in 1879 and Alice Hoschedé had become his partner, adding to his two sons her six children by her late husband.

From his first year in Giverny, Monet pursued a new theme. Many of the haystack studies of this period, and the later series of grain stacks, were painted around this mostly agricultural area. In both groups of pictures, in keeping with the main aim of Impressionism, Monet concentrated on capturing the effect of light at a particular time of day, paying close attention to the surprising and beautiful range of colors he found in the subject.

1884
26" x 32"
Oil on canvas
Pushkin Museum, Moscow

Woman with a Parasol

Monet painted three similar portraits of a lady with a parasol. The first painting lovingly portrays Camille with Jean in 1875. The other two, of which this, *Woman with a Parasol, Turned to the Left*, is one, were painted in 1886 and reveal how strongly Camille's image persisted in Monet's mind seven years after her premature death. These two works form a pair: in the second the parasol is turned to the right, throwing different light onto the face and figure. Monet used bold brushstrokes to show that the clouds were moving fast on a windy day.

The subject here was one of Monet's stepdaughters, Suzanne Hoschedé, posing near their home at Giverny. Tragically, like Camille, she also died young, at thirty-one. Monet cherished the portraits of her until his death.

1886
52" x 35"
Oil on canvas
Musée d'Orsay, Paris

Storm, Belle-Ile Coast

Forever searching for fresh subjects, in the fall of 1866 Monet visited Brittany and discovered the fearsome challenge of Belle-Ile's rocky coastline. With few tourists around, he painted unhindered – except by the lashing rains and high winds that snatched his brush and palette from his hands. It was precisely the drama of storm-tossed seas that Monet wanted to capture, so he persisted day after day, securing his easel with ropes and stones. For over two months he lodged in a fisherman's house, eating little but seafood at the village inn. Thirty-nine canvases were painted, including this one, where violent colors mirror the powerful clash of sea and rocks, and a high horizon intensifies the stormy turmoil.

1886
26" x 32"
Oil on canvas
Musée d'Orsay, Paris

The Boat at Giverny

Monet loved to be on or near water, and, better still, to be painting afloat. At Argenteuil, most likely in 1873, he built a floating studio by adding a tall cabin to a modest vessel. Paintings by Manet, John Singer Sargent and Monet himself show the artist at work in his studio boat. Ten years later, on settling in Giverny, one of the first things Monet did was to build a boathouse for the studio boat, his pair of sculls and his *norvegiénne*. It is from the last, a high-prowed skiff, that Blanche, Suzanne and Germaine Hoschedé, Monet's stepdaughters, are seen fishing. The water, much as the girls, was Monet's subject. Often, it was told, he would stand for minutes at a time, transfixed by the play of light in the transparent depths of his beloved waterlily pond.

1887
39" x 51"
Oil on canvas
Musée d'Orsay, Paris

A n t i b e s

Capturing the quality of natural light was a lifelong quest for Monet, so it was inevitable that he should grapple with the pure, intense light of the Mediterranean. In 1884 he painted on the Italian Riviera at Bordighera, before working his way westwards along the French coast. What he achieved bounced him between elation and despair.

Then, in the spring of 1888, he stayed for three months on the Côte d'Azur. At Antibes he was again overwhelmed by the clear, luminous southern light. "Everything is blue, pink and gold," he wrote. "You swim in blue air, it's frightful." This time Monet felt better equipped, and in June he showed ten Antibes canvases, including this one, at the Boussod & Valadon gallery. They all sold, mainly to American buyers.

1888
26" x 36"
Oil on canvas
Courtauld Institute Galleries, London

Grain Stacks, End of Summer

In the late summer of 1890, walking in the field overlooked by his studio, Monet was struck by the way local farmers protected the grain stacks from the weather by covering them with hay. Intending at first to paint the scene in both bright sun and cloud, he soon realized that subtle changes in the light lent it far more potential than he could exploit in just two pictures. To solve the problem, he decided to take several canvases into the field and work on one in the morning, then, when the light changed at noon, turn to another portraying that time of day, and so on.

Monet was able to concentrate on his *Grain Stacks* series until the spring of 1891. Fifteen of the paintings were shown in May 1891, winning him much praise and earning him enough money to buy the house he had been renting at Giverny.

1890-1
24" x 40"
Oil on canvas
Musée d'Orsay, Paris

Poplars on the Epte

After the grain stacks, the poplars lining the banks of the Epte at Limetz, near Monet's house in Giverny, provided the subject of his second major series of paintings. Soon after starting work he discovered that the trees were to be felled and auctioned. Having failed to persuade the local mayor to postpone the sale, Monet agreed to pay the keenest buyer the difference between what the man was prepared to pay and the successful bid. His condition was that the trees should not be cut until he had painted them. The deal was struck and from the spring until the autumn of 1891 Monet devoted himself to his subject, working in every kind of light from his studio boat on the river. As ever, his aim was to "paint directly from nature," to capture the most fleeting effects of light and color.

1891
37" x 29"
Oil on canvas
Tate Gallery, London

Rouen Cathedral

During February 1892, and again in 1893, Monet worked on twenty pictures of the passage of light across the weathered facade of Rouen's Gothic cathedral. This canvas, *Rouen Cathedral, Harmony in Blue and Gold, Morning Sun*, shows it in full sunlight, but no two are the same. In fact they reveal how wide a range of lighting effects could be seen from almost the same viewpoint in Monet's temporary studio over a milliner's shop.

"I'm painting like a madman," he wrote in 1893. "I'm completely finished and now I'm good for nothing else." Relying on memory, he continued the series at Giverny, finishing it in 1894. All twenty works were exhibited in Paris the following year to great acclaim – indeed, such was Monet's reputation by this time that there were offers to buy paintings sight unseen.

1894
43" x 29"
Oil on canvas
Musée d'Orsay, Paris

Waterlilies, Harmony in Green

After an intense struggle with the authorities, Monet won permission in 1893 to make a water garden out of a pond on land he had bought just outside his garden at Giverny. With its waterlilies and other aquatic plants, and its elegant wooden bridge, this watery domain became an endless source of inspiration to Monet, both as an artist and a gardener.

Although he had painted the Japanese bridge in 1895, it was not until four years later that Monet devoted a series of canvases to it. Ten, including this picture, were exhibited in 1900 and had a superb reception – even Edgar Degas, although not usually a great admirer of Monet, wanted to buy one of the *Waterlily* series.

1899
35" x 37"
Oil on canvas
Musée d'Orsay, Paris

The Houses of Parliament, Sunset

After about 1890 Monet painted mainly landscapes, or more accurately, the effects of light and the weather on a scene. London, with its rain, its mist and above all its smog, was a fertile ground, and over some thirty years the painter became very fond of it. On his final visit, in 1901, he worked on dozens of paintings at the same time, making pastel drawings as references to help him finish the canvases back in Giverny. This explains why some of the London pictures have dates after 1901. Monet was particularly fascinated by the Houses of Parliament, which he painted many times in both dense fog and hazy sunsets. In these works, London has a brooding feel, reminiscent of a Dickens novel.

1903
33" x 36"
Oil on canvas
National Gallery of Art, Washington D.C.
(Chester Dale Collection)

Blue Waterlilies

As early as 1890 Monet had feared that his attempts to paint the quality of water "will drive me mad...." He nevertheless went on to paint his waterlily pond 236 times, right up to his death over thirty years later.

Soon after the First World War, the painter and his friend the French statesman Georges Clemenceau conceived the idea of a series of waterlily paintings to be donated to the French nation as a peace memorial. It was decided that the works were to be displayed in a room at the Orangerie of the Tuileries in Paris – this painting is from one of the sections there. Though it was "finished" in 1922, the series was not moved from Giverny until 1926, as Monet, aware of the importance of these paintings, wanted them near him to retouch and revise at his leisure.

1916-19
79" x 79"
Oil on canvas
Musée d'Orsay, Paris

*A*cknowledgements

....

The publishers would like to thank the following
for permission to reproduce:–

Art Resource, New York, for the title page, the
last page, the back flap, pp. 10-11, 12-13,
14, 26-27, 28-29, 30-31, 32-33, 37,
38-39, 42-43, 48-49, 51, 53, 54, 56-57;

The Bridgeman Art Library, London, for
pp. 18-19, 24-25 and 44-45 with thanks to
Giraudon, and pp. 46;

Copyright, Paris, for the jacket and
pp. 17, 20-21, 22-23, 34-35, 59;

and the Musée d'Orsay, Paris, and the Musée
Marmottan, Paris.

Title page and facing page:
Camille on the Beach (detail)
Musée Marmottan, Paris